Jaguars

By Julie Guidone

Reading Consultant: Susan Nations, M.Ed.,
author/literacy coach/consultant in literacy development

WEEKLY READER®
PUBLISHING

Please visit our web site at **www.garethstevens.com**.
For a free catalog describing our list of high-quality books,
call 1-800-542-2595 (USA) or 1-800-387-3178 (Canada).
Our fax: 1-877-542-2596

Library of Congress Cataloging-in-Publication Data

Guidone, Julie.
    Jaguars / Julie Guidone.
        p. cm. — (Animals that live in the rain forest)
      Includes bibliographical references and index.
      ISBN-10: 1-4339-0023-8   ISBN-13: 978-1-4339-0023-5 (lib. bdg.)
      ISBN-10: 1-4339-0105-6   ISBN-13: 978-1-4339-0105-8 (softcover)
      1. Jaguar—Juvenile literature. I. Title.
    QL737.C23G84   2009
    599.75'5—dc22   2008029046

This edition first published in 2009 by
Weekly Reader® Books
An Imprint of Gareth Stevens Publishing
1 Reader's Digest Road
Pleasantville, NY 10570-7000 USA

Copyright © 2009 by Gareth Stevens, Inc.

Executive Managing Editor: Lisa M. Herrington
Senior Editor: Barbara Bakowski
Creative Director: Lisa Donovan
Designers: Michelle Castro, Alexandria Davis
Photo Researcher: Diane Laska-Swanke
Publisher: Keith Garton

Photo Credits: Cover © Shutterstock; pp. 1, 5, 9 (top and inset), 21 © Michael & Patricia Fogden/
Minden Pictures; p. 7 © SA Team/Foto Natura/Minden Pictures; p. 9 (bottom and inset) © Gregory
G. Dimijian/Photo Researchers, Inc.; p. 11 © Photos.com/Jupiterimages Unlimited; pp. 13, 17 © Nick
Gordon/naturepl.com; p. 15 © andy rouse-wildlife/Alamy; p. 19 © Pete Oxford/Minden Pictures

Printed in the United States of America

1 2 3 4 5 6 7 8 9 10 09 08

Table of Contents

Boldface words appear in the glossary.

Big Cats

Jaguars are big cats.
They live in **rain forests** in
Central and South America.
Rain forests are warm,
wet woodlands.

Baby jaguars are called kittens. A kitten stays with its mother for one to two years.

People sometimes confuse jaguars with leopards. Can you tell the difference? The large spots on the jaguar's fur have smaller spots inside them.

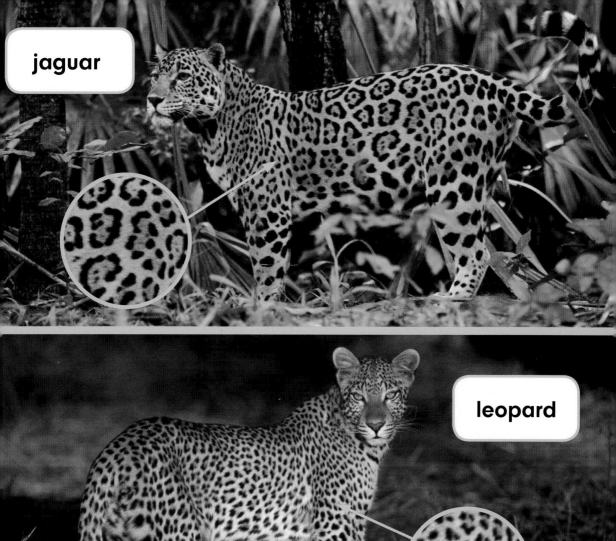

jaguar

leopard

9

Hunting and Swimming

Jaguars eat almost anything they can catch. Sometimes they climb trees to hunt monkeys and sloths.

Jaguars often hunt close to rivers. They pull fish, turtles, and alligators from the water.

turtle

Jaguars use their strong jaws and sharp teeth to eat **prey**. Prey are animals that are killed for food.

jaw

teeth

Jaguars are strong swimmers. They bathe, rest, and play in rain forest streams.

Save the Jaguars

Jaguars are **endangered**. They are at risk of dying out. People kill jaguars that try to eat farm animals. People also kill jaguars for their fur.

Areas of the rain forest have been cleared for farms. Jaguars do not have as much land as they need. People are working to protect the rain forests and the jaguars.

Glossary

endangered: in danger of dying out completely

prey: animals that are killed for food

rain forests: warm, rainy woodlands with many types of plants and animals

For More Information

Books

Cats That Roar! Hello Reader (series).
Kimberly Weinberger (Cartwheel, 2002)

Jaguars: World's Strongest Cats. Dangerous Cats (series).
Amelie von Zumbusch (Rosen Publishing, 2007)

Web Sites

Defenders of Wildlife: Jaguar
www.defenders.org/wildlife_and_habitat/wildlife/jaguar.php
Read facts about jaguars. You can even listen to a jaguar roar!

Enchanted Learning: All About Rainforests
www.enchantedlearning.com/subjects/rainforest
Learn more about rain forests and the animals that live there.

Index

About the Author

Julie Guidone has taught kindergarten and first and second grades in Madison, Connecticut, and Fayetteville, New York. She loves to take her students on field trips to the zoo to learn about all kinds of animals! She lives in Syracuse, New York, with her husband, Chris, and her son, Anthony.